HOW TO LIVE A SUCCESSFUL LIFE WITH GOD

STANLEY LONG

HEARING GOD

Hearing God is important, especially at those great moments in life. If you have a hard time hearing God, you might want to consider some very vital basics.

- *Don't go to God for quick fixes.*
  Your relationship with God is the key to hearing Him speak to you. The object of prayer is intimacy, not quick answers.

- *Don't ask unless you're willing to accept God's answers.*
  Don't ask for guidance unless you are willing to accept it. God is not interested in showing you His will just for your consideration.

- *Don't expect God to shout.*
  Learning to be quiet is essential to effective listening. You can't jam your mind with carnal influences 12 hours a day and expect God to reveal His plans for you during a commercial.

- *Watch out for a plug on the line.*
  If you are, passively or openly, rebelling against God in some area of your life, you are putting a plug in the prayer pipeline that God uses to deliver His messages.

- *Be willing to be God's fool.*
  God gave us common sense, and most of the time He expects us to use it. His will makes sense to our reason and intelligence. But every now and then, He will cut across human reason and totally go contrary to it. If we are willing to be His fool, we will be amazed by His power.

- *Don't miss the continuity between God and His Word.*
  God's guidance will never go against the principles of Scripture. His will is always consistent with His revealed will in His Word.

ADJUST

We can improve our relationships with just a little bit of adjustment. If we work at giving compliments rather than complaints, it will surprise us how much we can influence another person's behavior and do wonders for the atmosphere.

When we compliment people with words of appreciation and affection, it projects acceptance and creates trust and security. Compliments can head off wars before they start and encourage people to keep trying.

For example, what if you told your teen, spouse, or sibling, "You do a great job with the lawn (yard, dishes, etc.)," "You look great, even in your old sweats!" or "It really feels great to be with you"? What if you said, "Thanks for being a great dad (mom) to our kids" or "Thanks for taking out the garbage"?

For some reason, we feel that people don't deserve a compliment for doing what we think they are supposed to do. We could change the atmosphere in our homes instantly if we changed that kind of thinking. In fact, we could turn our environments into seas of gladness with just a few minor adjustments.

What would happen in your home if you refuse to pick at one another over petty annoyances? What would happen if, before you criticize, you ask yourself, "How important is this issue, really?" What might happen if you ask yourself, "Is this comment going to help or hurt our relationship?" or "Is the issue at stake more important than the relationship?"

Isn't it much wiser to choose what you say than to say what you choose?

The Bible says, "*Wherefore, my beloved brethren, let every man be swift to hear, slow to speak, slow to wrath*" (James 1:19).

LISTEN

The famous preacher and writer, Phillips Brooks penned some intriguing words in his famous hymn, "*O Little Town of Bethlehem*." Ponder the point of the 3rd stanza:

> *How silently, how silently, the*
> *wondrous Gift is given!*
>
> *So God imparts to human hearts the*
> *blessings of His heaven.*
>
> *No ear may hear His coming, but in*
> *this world of sin,*
>
> *Where meek souls will receive Him*
> *still, the dear Christ enters in.*

Does God often speak silently?

Think about this: "*And he said, Go forth, and stand upon the mount before the Lord. And, behold, the Lord passed by, and a great and strong wind rent the mountains, and brake in pieces the rocks before the*

Lord; but the Lord was not in the wind: and after the wind an earthquake; but the Lord was not in the earthquake: And after the earthquake a fire; but the Lord was not in the fire: and after the fire a still small voice" (1 Kings 19:11-12).

Would you hear God if He spoke to you in a gentle whisper?

TIME

Life is short and fragile. From one day to the next, we never know what will interrupt our daily routine. That's why it's so important that we weigh our daily choices. Every choice matters—from what we eat to what we say. We must slow down enough to question our choices and to consider what is truly important.

What is it that we really want to get out of life in the time we have left?

Consider these thought generators:

- God loves you very much, and He wants to be a part of the choices you make.

- Ask God for His wisdom. Be faithful to what He shows you and what you know to be in harmony with His will.

- Remember, any day may be your last. Make life investments that have eternal returns.

PRODUCE

God's Word clearly teaches us that He wants us to lead productive lives. "Productive" is an interesting word. It needs defining; and since He made us, God is the best one to determine what is and what isn't a productive life.

Here are, however, some basic steps which we can take to be productive, even by God's standards:

- CULTIVATE roots deep in the soil of God's Word (see Psalm 1). Otherwise, you will be spiritual tumbleweed.

- ELIMINATE the "weeds" in your life. Uproot anything that saps your time, energy, and money, or that prevents you from bearing spiritual fruit (see Galatians 5:19-26).

- COOPERATE with God's pruning. He lops off branches that don't produce (and some that do) to lead to even greater crops (see John 15:1-6).

- WAIT for the harvest. You must abide in Him to produce fruit (see 1 Corinthians 3:6-8). Even then, it takes time for the fruit to ripen.

- REJOICE in your productivity (see Galatians 6:8-10).

QUESTION

When a person does something nice for you, it's difficult to dislike that individual. When folks go out of their way to show us love, it makes it hard not to at least act in a friendly fashion toward those persons. So, what happens in a church when a great many people regularly complete secret acts of Christian love?

ANSWER

The answer is obvious: Everyone has to be nice to everybody else because no one knows who is responsible for showing the love received! A wonderful atmosphere exists when the whole congregation gets excited about lavishing God's love upon others.

TESTIFY

When you read the Bible, it is very clear that God expects us to tell others who do not know Him just what He has done for us. God's love for the world is so great that He wants everyone to enjoy the same privilege of having a meaningful relationship with Him.

There are many ways to witness for Christ, but one very important way is to witness with our lives. Our ways must back up our words.

Consider the following story: One morning, centuries ago, the famous St. Francis of Assisi said to a brother monk, "Let us go down into the town and preach." The two of them walked slowly along the road and eventually reached the town. They walked through the main streets and the side streets and even made their way out into the suburbs. St. Francis, however, did not stop anywhere for a preaching appointment but gradually guided them back from the town toward the monastery. Presently, his companion asked if he had forgotten the preaching. St. Francis replied, "We were preaching while we were walking. We have been seen by many, and our behavior has been closely watched. It was in this way that we preached our morning sermon. My brother, it is no use walking anywhere to preach unless we preach everywhere we walk."

It is true: What we do speaks louder than what we say. So, let's show *and* tell. Show a life that God has had an impact upon and tell the story of His grace at work in our lives.

God has done great things for us. Let's not be ashamed or afraid to testify so that others may have hope in the midst of the challenging realities of life. Remember this:

- You will face situations that will test your faith. Respond to them in obedience to God and grow closer to Him.

- When God asks you to do something, don't shrink back in fear. Do it.

- Each day, live in a way that shows non-Christians how a person transformed by Christ behaves. You may never get another chance to show them.

- Don't waste your resources of time and energy on that which brings you nothing valuable in return. Value these resources and use them wisely.

- Don't let disappointments destroy your peace. It's not the end of the world.

- Pursue a mission rather than an ambition. Make your life count, one day at a time.

HOT/COLD

A story is told about a typical church meeting room where the thermostat was located near the door. When someone came in and felt a bit chilly, he or she would go to the thermostat and turn it up. Then someone else would come in, perhaps perspiring from a brisk walk, and immediately turn the thermostat down.

One day, the pastor was orienting a new custodian to the bright and shiny thermostat. The pastor said with a sly wink, "That thermostat is purely ornamental. It's not connected to anything. The real controls are back here in the closet." Opening a closet door, he continued, "Here is the thermostat that is wired to the heating system."

No matter who we are, there are always people around us who want us to be "warmer" or "cooler"—people who are trying to get us to march to their drumbeat. Jesus, however, was able to hear those around Him, but He was not controlled by them. He was marching

to a different drumbeat. The magnetic authority
and power of Jesus comes from the fact that He was
connected to the Unseen Power Source, and He was
not influenced by the demands of other people—not
even by His close friends. This was how Jesus kept
focus for His life. He could say "Yes!" to the Father
and "No" to the lure of others' agendas because of His
connection to the Source.

When we begin to learn to march to God's drumbeat,
we will find that we are aligned to heaven's purpose
and power, and we will have a clear direction for our
lives, even though it may conflict with the agendas
others have.

WATCH OUT

Satan's ploy is to rob and steal from our relationships and from us. Sometimes he will even use things that appear to be good to steal from you that which would be best. Other times it's not Satan at all but just our thoughtlessness that hurts us. Watch out for these:

- Having too many individualized activities— Going in opposite directions too many days and nights can take its toll on a relationship.

- Not scheduling time for togetherness—If you don't schedule time you probably won't find time. Take time for each other.

- Not communicating regularly or meaningfully—We have to work at communicating in order to maintain close bonds in the midst of busyness.

- Not resolving differences that arise—
  Intimacy is easier to destroy than it is to
  build. Deal with your issues.

- Communicating in a hurtful way—Ask
  yourself, "Do my words invite in or do they
  push away?" Never attack a person; always
  attack the issue. Speak kindly.

- Dishonesty—Being dishonest always hurts.
  Deception never helps. Tell the truth.

- Nagging—Once you have plainly said
  something and you know it's been heard,
  drop it. Encourage one another.

- Behaving abusively—Abusive behavior is
  damaging to the spirit and the soul, as well
  as the body. Treat one another in love.

- Being unfaithful—Nothing hurts a
  relationship like infidelity. Temporary
  excitement will never be worth the agony.

FIGHT BACK

A good steward not only manages his or her money well, but also manages life well. If it feels like someone other than you is in control of your life, it might be a good time to look at the reason.

If your life feels too busy and you are on overload, this might be a good time to reassess. Activity overload is a toxic condition. It takes away the pleasure of anticipation, the delight of reminiscing, the joy of friendship, and ultimately leads to exhaustion.

Here are some ideas to help you fight back:

- Reestablish control of your life and schedule. Do some self-examination and intentional correction. Change is yours if you want it bad enough.

- Prioritize activities and commitments. Let the Word of God determine your priorities. Look at things from a godly perspective. Remember that people are more important than things.

- Practice saying no. Remember that this is not an excuse for noninvolvement, laziness, or insensitivity. It is simply a mechanism for living by your priorities and allowing God to direct your life rather than allowing the world to direct it.

- Preserve your vitality for the things that really matter.

- Protect open spaces. Don't saturate your schedule.

- Prune your activities. All activities should come up for periodic review, evaluation, and justification of their continued existence.

- Restore the practice of Sabbath rest.

COMMUNICATE

C ommunication continues to be one of the premier problems in our society today. Whether in our homes or on our jobs, we struggle to be heard by and to hear others. Jesus didn't have that problem. He communicated with the world in such a way that His words and ideas are still with us today, 2000 years later.

There are, however, some basic principles that might help us communicate better. We can implement these principles in our own lives. Consider these thoughts from Clement Communications and see how close they are to what Jesus did:

- Don't talk so much. You can't listen if you're carrying the conversation.

- Persuade the other person to keep talking. Ask probing questions.

- Nod your head and maintain eye contact. Don't interrupt or finish the other person's sentences.

- Pay complete attention. Concentrate. Don't think about what you'll say next. Listen for keys to others' interests. Ask questions that will identify wants and desires.

- Concentrate on ideas, not just facts. Try to understand the deeper needs of the speaker.

- Watch the body language. Expressions, nervous actions, and inflections of voice can tell you what words won't.

- Control your emotions. If accused or antagonized, keep an open mind and stay relaxed.

- Take notes. Don't trust important information to memory.

- Get feedback. To avoid misunderstandings, repeat back to people what they have said as you understand it. Listen to how they correct your incorrect perceptions.

JOIN US

Let us turn our thoughts toward opening our heart's door to friends and strangers. One example is the Christmas story. The Christmas story is full of visits from strangers and friends. To get started, ponder these questions:

- Name as many visitors as you can. How many can you remember?

- If a young couple like Mary and Joseph came to your door looking for shelter, would you welcome them? Why or why not?

- What are some of the reasons that we hesitate to invite others to join us in our Christmas activities?

- What good things do friends offer to us when we open our hearts and homes?

- What good things might a stranger bring to our Christmas celebrations?

- Jesus was a stranger here on earth when He arrived in human form. What kinds of people did God choose to welcome Him?

- What did these choices say about the kind of ruler He would become?

Ponder this:

"If someone listens, or stretches out a hand, or whispers a kind word of encouragement, or attempts to understand a lonely person, extraordinary things begin to happen."

—Loretta Girzartis

LOOK INSIDE

L ife is, oh, so short. We often fail to get out of life all that we can because of what we do to ourselves. Many of us don't even realize that the problem is us. We are the ones who get in the way of what we want in life; it's not other people, society, or our parents. There are some signals of self-sabotage, if we are alert enough to see them.

- Failure to accept responsibility for the direction of one's own life—It's silly to pass the blame. We have to take ownership of the decisions we make and their consequences. It's a fact: Choices today will affect tomorrow.

- Lack of people skills—Studies show that people who are happy and successful know how to get along with other people. Interpersonal skills account for 87 percent of why people get hired and stay employed; experience and product knowledge only matter 13 percent. Some of us seem to be born with this social ability. The rest of us have to learn it. Learn it we must, or we will cheat ourselves out of life's riches.

- Double mindedness—Lack of focus results in scattered thoughts. Scattered thoughts result in scattered activities. Scattered activities can result in a lack of progress toward any goal. We won't make it if our decisions are half-hearted and conceived without care. Ask yourself some tough "What will happen if . . . ?" questions.

- Wasting time—Time is an irretrievable, valuable resource. If we waste it, we lose it forever. Organization and prioritizing are the only means of maintaining balance between spiritual pursuits, work, and rest. Remember, life is 10 percent what happens to a person and 90 percent how the person reacts to what happens.

Don't sabotage yourself. Let God's dream for you become a reality.

SECULAR VS. SACRED

Recently, I purchased a new version of *The Message: The Prophets* by Eugene H. Peterson, a contemporary paraphrase of the Old Testament prophecies. I was so moved by the opening paragraphs in the introduction that I just had to share it.

> *"One of the bad habits that we pick up early in our lives is separating things and people into secular and sacred. We assume that the secular is what we are more or less in charge of: our jobs, our time, our money, our opinions, our entertainment, our government, our house and land, our social relations. The sacred is what God has charge of: worship and the Bible, heaven and hell, church and prayers. We then contrive to set aside a sacred place for God, designed, we say, to honor God but really intended*

*to keep God in his place, leaving us
free to have the final say in everything
else that goes on outside that space.*

*Prophets will have none of this. They
hold that everything, absolutely
everything, takes place on sacred
ground. God has something to say
about every aspect of our lives, the
way we feel and act in the so-called
privacy of our hearts and homes, the
way we make our money and the way
we spend it, the politics we embrace,
the wars we fight, the catastrophes
we endure, the people we hurt and
the people we help. Nothing is hid
from the scrutiny of God; nothing is
exempt from the rule of God; nothing
escapes the purposes of God."*[1]

Ponder that!

1 Eugene H. Peterson, The Message: The Prophets.
Colorado Springs, Colo.: NavPress, ©2000.

THE GOOD LIFE

One of the greatest challenges we face today is distinguishing between what the culture tells us is the "good life" and the "good life" as seen by God. The consumer- oriented culture that dominates our world says that the "good life" comes from making lots of money and projecting a successful image with all the toys and trappings that go along with it. But God defines success differently.

To live "the good life" God's way, we should:

- Seek wisdom, compassion, and freedom rather than appearance, affluence, and achievement.

- Remember that you were made in God's image, which is far more important than someone else's image of you.

- Make lifestyle choices that reflect good stewardship of God's gifts to you.

- Think of the world not so much as a marketplace, but as a community of people; and ask how you can contribute to the community rather than just take from it.

- Give up personal pursuits that interfere with your relationship with God.

- Listen compassionately to others, and act with compassion to help meet their needs.

- Face the tragedies of life with courage and hope.

- Make time for regular prayer, rest, relaxation, and worship.

When we do these things, we are getting closer to what true success looks like.

FLY HIGH

Did you know that an eagle knows when a storm is approaching, long before the storm breaks? The eagle will fly to some high point and wait for the storm winds to arrive. When the storm hits, the eagle sets its wings so that the wind lifts it up. While the storm rages below, the eagle is soaring above. The eagle does not escape the storm. It simply uses the storm to lift itself higher. It rises on the winds that bring the storm.

When the storms of life come upon us—and all of us will experience storms—we can rise above them by setting our minds and our faith upon God. The storms of life do not have to overcome us. We can allow God's power to lift us above them. God enables us to ride the winds of the storms that bring sickness, tragedy, failure, and disappointment into our lives. We, like the eagle, can soar above the storm.

Remember, it is not the burdens of life that weigh us down; it is how we respond to and handle them. The

Bible says, "*But those who hope in the* LORD *will renew their strength. They will soar on wings like eagles; they will run and not grow weary, they will walk and not be faint*" (Isaiah 40:31, NIV).

KEEP SWINGING

M any of the greatest players in baseball have gotten off to a slow start. For example, Willie Mays got only one hit in his first 26 at-bats in the majors. He went on to hit 660 home runs and racked up more than a dozen distinguished honors. Hank Aaron went zero for four in his major league debut. He now holds the all-time home run title.

These legends of the game teach us a vital lesson: A strong finish is more important than a strong beginning. In baseball—as in life—one-hit wonders are a dime a dozen; but those who go the distance are one in a million. A strong finish requires something more than luck, and even more than talent. It requires persistence.

The Apostle Paul realized that consistent and long-term faithfulness to his mission would determine the value of his ministry, not the occasional flash of brilliance. For this reason, he said, "*But I keep under my body, and bring it into subjection: lest that by any means, when I have preached to others, I myself should be a castaway"* (1 Corinthians 9:27).

GUIDANCE

One of the members of a certain church thoughtfully shared with me a beautiful insight on guidance. The author is unknown. It is so enjoyable that I want to share it with you:

> *When I meditated on the word "guidance," I kept seeing "dance" at the end of the word. I remembered reading that doing God's will is a lot like dancing. When two people try to dance together and both attempt to lead, nothing feels right. Their movement doesn't flow with the music; everything is quite uncomfortable and jerky. When one person relaxes and lets the other lead, both bodies begin to flow with the music. One gives gentle cues, perhaps with a nudge to the back or by pressing lightly in one direction*

or another. It's as if two become one body, moving beautifully. The dance takes surrender, willingness, and attentiveness from one person and gentle guidance and skill from the other.

My eyes were drawn back to the word "guidance." When I saw the letter "g," I thought of God followed by "u" and "i." God, "u" and "I" dance. God, you and I dance; this statement is what guidance means to me. As I lowered my head, I became willing to trust that I would get guidance about my life. Once again, I became willing to let God lead.

STRENGTH

Jesus makes it very clear that the way up is down. H said, "*He that is greatest among you, let him.. serve*" (Luke 22:26). This is a concept that Jesus taught and practiced. But where do we get the strength to pull that off? We get it from God Himself.

Note God's promises:

"*Not by might, nor by power, but by my spirit, saith the Lord of hosts*" (Zechariah 4:6b).

"*O God, thou art terrible out of thy holy places: the God of Israel is he that giveth strength and power unto his people. Blessed be God*" (Psalm 68:35).

"*Trust ye in the Lord for ever: for in the Lord Jehovah is everlasting strength*" (Isaiah 26:4).

"*Fear thou not; for I am with thee: be not dismayed; for I am thy God: I will strengthen thee; yea, I will help thee; yea, I will uphold thee with the right hand of my righteousness*" (Isaiah 41:10).

"For it is God which worketh in you both to will and to do of his good pleasure" (Philippians 2:13).

"I can do all things through Christ which strengtheneth me" (Philippians 4:13).

"The righteous also shall hold on his way, and he that hath clean hands shall be stronger and stronger" (Job 17:9).

GOD'S PLANS

When we are placed upon this planet, God has a mission— an assignment—for each of us to complete. To get us there, He will often lead us down the most unexpected routes. For example, when one boy was 7-years-old, his family was forced out of their home on a legal technicality, and he had to work to help support them.

At age 9, his mother died. At 22, he lost his job as a store clerk. He wanted to go to law school, but his educational preparation wasn't good enough. At 23, he went into debt to become a partner in a small store.

At age 26, his business partner died, leaving him with a huge debt that took years to repay. At 28, after courting a girl for four years, he asked her to marry him; but she said, "No." At 37, on his third try, he was elected to Congress; but two years later, he failed to be reelected.

At 41, his 4-year-old son died. At 45, he ran for the Senate and lost. At 47, he failed as the vice-presidential candidate. At 49, he ran for the Senate again, and lost. At 51, he ran for the presidency of the United States. His name was Abraham Lincoln.

Defeats, setbacks, rejections, detours, and the like do not mean that God is not leading us into fulfilling His purpose for our lives.

REKINDLE

If you find that your marriage is stagnating or you are too tired to keep the spark of romance alive, you need help.

Marriage requires effort to make it vibrant and enduring. Sometimes it means listening to your spouse when you'd rather go to sleep, hanging up that wet towel yet again, and yes, taking out the garbage. Putting your partner first through daily little acts of kindness will help you treasure your marriage.

Here are some ideas on how to keep your marriage alive:

- Listen to your spouse.

- Look for ways to serve,
  not for ways to be served.

- Develop a friendship with your spouse. Men value doing things together. Women value talking together. Why not combine both and foster quality time together?

- Keep dating your mate.

- Be silly. Write notes, poems, give gag gifts, and consistently encourage one another.

- Make a prayer list together and write in the answers to those prayers. Let your relationship with God foster closeness with your mate.

- Adopt a daily sharing time. Set a regular time each day when the two of you can spend time alone together, sharing.

- Do something for others together. Help an elderly neighbor, be an uncle or an aunt to a single-parent child, teach a Sunday school class at church, etc.

- Develop the encouragement habit. Give support and comfort during the mundane day-to-day stuff.

- Decide to think positively, and determine that your marriage will be an adventure and a delight.

PATIENCE

Patience is one of the choice qualities of the human spirit. Consider these 10 perspectives:

- Patience is needed with everyone, but first of all with ourselves.

- Quiet patience can and does master and outlive all boisterous, stormy, human discord.

- The key to everything is patience. You get the chicken by hatching the egg, not by smashing the egg open.

- The lovely thing about patience is that it annoys the person that is annoying you.

- Patience and understanding are companions to contentment.

- Be patient with the faults of others; they may have to be patient with yours.

- Nothing worthwhile ever happens in a hurry—so be patient!

- Patience strengthens the spirit, sweetens the temper, stifles anger, subdues pride, and bridles the tongue.

- Like farmers, we need to learn that we can't sow and reap in the same day.

- Many a man has turned and left the dock just before his ship came in.

PERSPECTIVE

One of the members of my church sent the following information to me last week, and it is just too good to keep to myself:

- If you own just one Bible, you are abundantly blessed. One-third of the entire world does not have access to one.

- If you woke up this morning with more health than illness, you are more blessed than the million people who will not survive this week.

- If you have never experienced the danger of battle, the loneliness of imprisonment, the agony of torture, or the pangs of starvation, you are ahead of 500 million people in the world.

- If you can attend a church meeting without fear of harassment, arrest, torture, or death, you are more blessed than three billion people in the world.

- If you have food in the refrigerator, clothes on your back, a roof over your head, and a place to sleep, you are richer than 75 percent of this world.

- If you have money in the bank, in your wallet, or spare change in a dish somewhere, you are among the top 8 percent of the world's wealthy.

- If your parents are still alive and still married, you belong to a very rare group, even in the United States.

- If you can read this page, you are more blessed than over two billion people in the world who cannot read at all.

We take so much for granted. May God forgive us and help us to be more grateful.

FUTURE OF LONELINESS

Relationships are crucial to our quality of life. We need them, and without them we will be extremely lonely people. Sometimes we turn people off without intending to do so. Sometimes people don't want to be around us, but we don't know why.

Avoiding these five relationship terminators will increase our chances of not being lonely:

- ORDERING—Giving orders or commands may, at times, be appropriate with children; but it will breed anger, fear, or resentment with other adults. Avoid making demanding statements like "Stop that!" and "You have to…"

- MORALIZING—Telling people when they ought to feel guilty or morally inferior will not win you any popularity contests. Avoid making statements that begin with "You shouldn't…" and "You ought…"

- LECTURING—People resent a parent-child communication style. It lowers their self-esteem while highlighting your supposed superiority.

- CRITICIZING—Criticism is often destructive to one's self-image, and it often causes ongoing conflict. Avoid phrases like "You are always..." and "You never…"

- ANALYZING—Watch out for any tendency to play amateur psychologist. Avoid jumping to conclusions like "You're only doing that to hurt me" or "Your smile only hides your hostility."

The Bible gives us some sound advice on how to make relationships work. It says: "*For all the law is fulfilled in one word, even in this; Thou shalt love thy neighbour as thyself*" (Galatians 5:14).

CHOOSE WELL

Whether we get what we want out of life has less to do with our circumstances and more to do with our choices. Every day, all day, God gives us the right to make our own choices. We can get much more out of our situations if we choose well.

Let me suggest:

- Choose a realistic, attainable goal that you want to accomplish in the next year, next 5 years, and next 10 years. Then choose a daily routine that will help you get there.

- Choose wisdom in responding to life. Godly wisdom is seeing life from God's perspective, and choosing to react to life in the way that God wants. Wisdom like that comes from the Bible and prayer.

- Choose to spend your time wisely. Don't schedule things that don't fit your priorities.

- Choose your battles. Save energy by fighting for that worth fighting for.

- Choose your words. Words build up or tear down, comfort or discourage, heal or hurt, make or break.

- Choose your friends. Select friends who love God, love you, and aren't afraid to tell you the truth. Friends hold you accountable to do what is right. Who are your four best friends? What effect are they having on you?

- Choose your attitude. Your choice can decide the outcome of your life. Negative thoughts have no power unless you empower them. Make a list of as many things that God has done for you as you can; and keep the list handy so that you can pull it out whenever a negative attitude tries to take over your mood.

PROSPERITY

The affluence of the American way of life is a mixed blessing. On the positive side, our prosperity has made life easier and has freed money to spread God's Word and do a lot of good. But on the negative side, prosperity requires so much of our time and attention. In fact, the urgency of our materialistic lifestyles becomes a tyranny that demands most of our energies—and more of us—than we really want to give.

I think the answer to this dilemma lies in three important motifs:

- ESTABLISH BALANCE—There must always be a balance in the area of material things. God does not have the same plan for any of us. What one family spends is different from another. We must seek to reach the balance between using material things and being controlled by material things in our own lives. To do this, a Christian must establish that Christ and His kingdom come first and all other considerations follow.

- CLARIFY YOUR FOCUS—For people who have committed themselves to higher values and an eternity with God, it is amazing how worldly our value system is. The real purpose of our resources is to use them to make a difference in our world. When the pursuit of things becomes our focus in life, there can be no doubt about whom we serve. Matthew 6:24 says that we can't serve two masters.

- SURRENDER TO GOD'S RULERSHIP— Nothing prohibits Christians from obeying God more than the tug of material comforts. Jesus frequently tested His followers by challenging their willingness to surrender everything for God's sake.

MONEY

It is important that we remember who the owner of everything really is. Our time, talent, and resources are, in fact, gifts from God. He has graciously provided guidelines concerning how we are to manage what He has loaned to us.

For example, when it comes to money, God tells us the following:

- DON'T WORRY ABOUT MONEY. Of all the things that Jesus could have said not to worry about, He specified finances. God promises to meet our material needs. Rest assured that He will.

- SET THE RIGHT PRIORITIES. Make God's kingdom and righteousness your first concern. Give. Do not let financial decisions consume your energy or time. Focus on the Lord, not your ledgers.

- BE DILIGENT AND RESPONSIBLE. Work hard and let God bless your productivity so that, with Him, you can meet your financial obligations.

- INVEST MONEY AND SEE IT GROW. The parable of the talents makes clear our obligation to use everything that God has given to us— including money—wisely. Invest it so that it will yield more. This will allow you to be a blessing to others.

- BE GENEROUS. As an act of worship, give to others as God has given to you in His goodness.

- RECOGNIZE THAT ALL YOU HAVE IS ON LOAN FROM GOD. As a responsible steward, ask God how He would have you to spend your money.

THE ABC'S OF FRIENDSHIP

A FRIEND:

A Accepts you as you are
B Believes in "you"
C Calls you just to say, "Hi"
D Doesn't give up on you
E Envisions the whole of you
   (even the unfinished parts)
F Forgives your mistakes
G Gives unconditionally
H Helps you
I Invites you over
J Just likes "being" with you
K Keeps you close-at-heart
L Loves you for who you are
M Makes a difference in your life
N Never judges
O Offers support
P Picks you up
Q Quiets your fears
R Raises your spirits
S Says nice things about you
T Tells you the truth when you need to hear it
U Understands you
V Values you
W Walks beside you
X Explains things you don't understand
Y Yells when you won't listen and
Z Zaps you back to reality

PRAYER

Prayer has changed more things than we can imagine. It has changed people, marriages, children, families, churches, businesses, governments, and nations, just to name a few things. Prayer can provide peace, joy, and healing. It can help open doors that are closed and even make your enemies behave. However, prayer is not magic; it does not work like some rabbit foot.

Here are five elements that will help your prayer work better for you:

- PRAYER TAKES TIME. Talking about it, reading about it, thinking about it— is not doing it. Don't kid yourself; it will take time.

- VALUE PRAYER. To pray, as God would like us to, is the greatest achievement on earth.

- ASK FOR HELP. To effect sufficient time in our daily schedules will require strength of purpose and deep dependence upon the Holy Spirit. Ask Him for help.

- PLUG THE LEAKS. Think of your days in terms of minutes—not hours—and make constructive use of each minute. John Wesley said that he divided his life into periods of five minutes and then endeavored to make each period count for God. Learn how to use those small increments of time for time with God.

- HONESTLY EXPOSE YOUR SOUL. When you do, you give God an opportunity to form His own image in it. God's acquaintance is not made hurriedly. Spend time with Him and it will change you and everything around you.

FINISH WELL

Through the years, I have enjoyed a very meaningful friendship with the president emeritus of World Vision International. Ted Engstrom is a very wise and humble man. He is retired now, but I will never forget a very practical illustration he tells about a flashlight.

He says, "*I was cleaning out a desk drawer when I found a flashlight I hadn't used in over a year. I flipped the switch but wasn't surprised when it gave no light. I unscrewed it and shook it to get the batteries out, but they wouldn't budge.*

"*Finally, after some effort, they came loose. What a mess! Battery acid had corroded the entire inside of the flashlight. The batteries were new when I'd put them in, and I'd stored them in a safe, warm place. But there was one problem. Those batteries weren't made to be warm and comfortable. They were designed to be turned on—to be used.*

"It is the same with us. We weren't created to be safe, warm, and comfortable. You and I were made to be 'turned on'—to put our love to work, to apply our patience in difficult, trying situations—to let our light shine." [2]

The Apostle Paul understood that a strong finish is more important than a strong beginning. Although his life had many outstanding moments, he considered his greatest achievement to be the fact that he, through God's grace, remained faithful to the end. Shortly before his death, he wrote these words: "I have fought a good fight, I have finished my course, I have kept the faith: Henceforth there is laid up for me a crown of righteousness, which the Lord, the righteous judge, shall give me at that day: and not to me only, but unto all them also that love his appearing" (2 Timothy 4:7-8).

Each project we undertake may not get off to a dynamic start. Some will fizzle and appear to be hopeless endeavors. Let's remember this: More valuable than quick success is long-term faithfulness.

A strong finish is more important than a strong beginning. Regardless of how we start, let's finish the race!

2 Engstrom's book The Pursuit of Excellence and in 750 Engaging Illustrations for Preachers, Teachers, and Writers edited by Craig Brian Larson